W0115304

ENDORSEMENTS

We must never overlook the fact that in a very real way, the ministry of ushers and greeters plays a critical role in facilitating the work of the Word and the Spirit in our services. Here's a tool you can use to be sure that those we entrust with the safety and overall security of the assembled members are well trained and focused on their work! I only wish this had been written sooner.

Lanre Asiru has written a relevant, and much needed guide to help every pastor who wants to see their church's core values and character clearly on display by ushers, greeters, and other staff, where first impressions are made. Inspired by years of personal experience, this volume is destined to meet a need in an important and often overlooked ministry of church!

It has been my pleasure to personally know the author as a friend and key team member of the church I pastor. I have witnessed for years the fruit of his ministry as the tested and proven precepts contained in these pages have been applied. Certainly, every usher and greeter ministry team member needs to be informed and equipped in the critical protocols contained in these pages. Expect your team to grow deeper and more fulfilled spiritually as well when they see themselves not simply as ushers but as "watchmen," "facilitators," and "ambassadors."

– David Munizzi
Lead Pastor, Catalyst International Church

It is my privilege to make commentary about this new book, Ushering In His Presence, *by Lanre Asiru. With knowledge of and experience in two distinct cultures, Lanre lays down biblical principles for an area of ministry that has received little, if any, literary attention. The tragedy of this lack is assumption that just any warm body with a few breaths in them can function as an usher.*

Training from this excellent volume will greet congregants, and most importantly, potential congregants with the love of God, proper finesse, and with that first impression that inspires a second visit— perhaps even a more in-depth association.

This writing is not theory, but a lifestyle and smile you could experience any Sunday morning at Lanre's home church. The author is there, practicing what he is herein preaching.

– Doug Maners
Lanre's former pastor

The first time I met Lanre Asiru, he was standing in the back of Catalyst International Church in Orlando, Florida. I remember seeing this tall, dignified man as he stood like a watchful soldier, looking over the congregation with a loving and protective gaze. I knew immediately that he was an usher, but he was not just handing out church bulletins or making sure kids stayed quiet. He took his job seriously. He knew he was a watchman in God's house.

I got to know Lanre after that day, and we immediately became friends because of our shared interest in his native Nigeria. I was not surprised to learn that he had written a book for people who serve as church ushers. Lanre is the best person I know to provide this training because ushering is not just a job to him. It is a holy calling. I believe your entire church leadership team would benefit from reading this helpful book, which teaches that all of God's ministers, regardless of their titles or positions, are called to be selfless servants.

– J. Lee Grady
Author and Director of The Mordecai Project

A MINISTRY MODEL
FOR SERVING IN
THE CHURCH

USHERING IN

His

PRESENCE

LANRE ASIRU

©2020 by Olanrewaju Asiru. All rights reserved.

Asiru, Olanrewaju

Ushering In His Presence: A Ministry Model for the Church

Paperback ISBN: 978-1-951492-42-7

Ebook ISBN: 978-1-951492-95-3

LOC Case # 1-9952266621

LOC Case#: 1-9664019031 Book Tribute Song

Publisher: HigherLife Development Services, Inc.

P.O. Box 623307 Oviedo, Florida 32762

(407) 563-4806 www.ahigherlife.com

No part of this book may be reproduced without written permission from the publisher or copyright holder, nor may any part of this book be transmitted in any form or by any means electronic, mechanical, photocopying, recording, or other, without prior written permission from the publisher or copyright holder unless otherwise noted scripture quotations taken from the Holy Bible, NEW INTERNATIONAL VERSION®, NIV® Copyright © 1973, 1978, 1984, 2011 by Biblica, Inc.® Used by permission. All rights reserved worldwide. Scripture quotations marked NKJV are taken from the New King James Version. Copyright © 1982 by Thomas Nelson, Inc. Used by permission. All rights reserved.

Scripture quotations marked ESV are from The Holy Bible, English Standard Version® (ESV®), copyright © 2001 by Crossway, a publishing ministry of Good News Publishers. Used by permission. All rights reserved.

Printed in the United States of America:

10 9 8 7 6 5 4 3 2 1   25 26 24 23 22 21

This book is dedicated to all true servants of God, ministering in one way or the other through service in churches all over the world. Know with assurance that your labor is not in vain.

– Olanrewaju (Lanre) Asiru

. . .

People are often unreasonable, irrational and self-centered;
Forgive them anyway.

If you are kind, people may accuse you of selfish, ulterior motives;
Be kind anyway.

If you are successful, you will win some unfaithful friends and some genuine enemies;
Succeed anyway.

If you are honest and sincere, people may deceive you;
Be honest and sincere anyway.

What you spend years creating, others could destroy overnight;
Create anyway.

If you find serenity and happiness, some may be jealous;
Be happy anyway.

The good you do today, will often be forgotten;
Do good anyway.

Give the best you have, and it may never be enough;
Give your best anyway.

In the final analysis, it is between you and God;
It was never between you and them anyway.

–Mother Teresa

CONTENTS

CONTENTS

INTRODUCTION

Often corporations provide a product or service with real value for many, yet for some reason, the public largely does not buy it. They might not even be aware of its existence. This is where marketing comes in, and why marketing is crucial for the sustenance and viability of any organization. It's no wonder then that corporations pay over a million dollars to place their commercials as part of the Super Bowl halftime show. The benefits far outweigh the cost. Simply put, these commercials help these corporations put their best foot forward, as the saying goes, by providing them limited seconds to project their image and products and services in the best possible light. Public relations departments exist within corporations that serve as their face, while simultaneously managing the corporation's brand.

Churches are no different than **for profit** corporations in this regard. While I have not encountered a church with a public relations department or ministry, churches also must accurately project who they are to each person who walks through their doors. First this is achieved through the usher ministry (sometimes called greeter, door holder, and other titles today), as these are the first persons to encounter church goers. Then what begins with the usher continues through other church ministry leaders and members.

Then, just as in the case of corporations, there are reasons why people seeking a church to call their home church, one where families can grow together, may or may not gravitate toward a church. Again, as in the case of unappreciated products and services, there are numerous churches worldwide that stand out, at least in terms of their building structures, as magnificent edifices; sights to behold, yet they remain empty in terms of attendance, fellowship, love, and in their fulfillment of the Great Commission. It is very easy to look outward and find external factors as the cause for certain challenges in life, when in reality, and with humility having its place in our hearts, we should be looking in the mirror, where truth can be found and revealed. The physical structure of a church will never be the true location of God's dwelling place. He desires to dwell in our hearts and to captivate us by His Holy Spirit.

For any church to be appealing to the public at large, it also must put its best foot forward. While there may not be a public relations department properly so called within churches, each church plays its part in "marketing" itself. Whether we admit it or not, every church invariably portrays itself as the best church out there for you; not in a way that puts down other churches (as one will find in the comical commercials between attorneys/law firms), but I am yet to visit any church's website that provides all the information you can imagine, portraying the church as full of love and the pastor then says, "But there's a better church down the street from us that I think has more love than us. I would recommend that church if you really want the full extent of God's love. We are however here for you. God bless you as you visit us."

Bottom line, each church can attempt to present itself in the best light possible, but as the saying goes, the proof of the pudding is in the eating. Whether or not the true nature and love of God exists within a church, as an example and representation of God's love, can only be felt by one's personal experience in that church; and not by the self-evaluated accolades eloquently stated on impressive church websites and other forms of social media. Regrettably, a critical aspect of all church services /events that isn't given enough attention and importance is the role of a church usher. This is an extremely sensitive position, regardless of the fact that it may be a volunteer position. Ushers, in a true sense, are the brand ambassadors of the church, invariably because they are the first point of contact for virtually anyone that visits a church. This makes their conduct, demeanor, and overall appearance a make-or-break factor as to whether or not the experience of a guest or even that of a regular member is a favorable one.

Here's the scenario a lot of pastors are oblivious to. They've preached a wonderful message; they see several new faces, and of course, every pastor has the hope and expectation that first-time guests will return. While the reason a significant number of first timers do not return to a particular church are varied and sometimes unknown, I do know for a fact and from personal experience, that some disservice is done through the conduct of the person the guest first encountered—the usher. Unfortunately for the poor pastor, he has no way of knowing what upset the guest, because it's rare for a first-time guest to schedule an appointment to meet with the pastor to voice dissatisfaction for the conduct of a certain usher or volunteer. Such a guest, even with the disappointment and hurt, will rationalize and say, "I'll just keep looking for a church that fits." Now, if it was a restaurant that overcooked a steak that was meant to be medium rare, you could ask to speak with a manager or give a bad review after leaving the restaurant. Again, it is highly unlikely (not impossible) anyone will give a church a bad review online. A church with improperly or inadequately trained ushers will continue to suffer growth stagnation because the interaction of guests and even regular members with an usher not fit for the position, will force an exodus of members and potential members on the church.

I like to put it this way, you could be the most angelic, loving, and giving person in a church, but even all these wonderful virtues don't necessarily make you suited for the worship team. If your singing voice makes dogs howl and cats go running for cover (you get my point). The role of a church usher isn't for everyone. There needs to be greater and more in-depth scrutiny into who serves in this capacity, and this is what this book attempts to address; not from a theoretical or text book approach, but from a biblical perspective and my personal experiences emanating from decades of ushering, by the mercy and grace of God and for His glory!

I believe this book provides revelatory insights and direction for church leadership, corporations at large, and anywhere there is the need to interact with people on a regular basis. The positioning of people as servers in a church setting in particular should no longer be seen as protocol; whereby a member or recent attendee desirous of serving is automatically placed on the ushering team because it's considered an easy fix for the zealous individual, which also frees the pastor or other leadership from the need to prayerfully meditate on the right fit for the individual, as led by the Spirit.

My prayer is that this book will be of value to every reader, such that there is a refocus on the necessities of building God's kingdom— not by might nor power, but by the Spirit of the Living God! May the Holy Spirit inspire and grant revelation to every reader, such that each person is used more than ever before, for God's glory!

CHAPTER ONE

WHO THEY ARE

You can't miss them! They're in every church in one capacity or another. Some are in uniforms, some regulate the dress code differently with men wearing matching jackets and women wear skirts at a certain length; some are more casual in their appearance, and some even wear gloves. While the focus is not (and should not be) on what they wear, one will find a commonality in their role within the church.

The words "usher" and "ushering" do not appear in the Bible, yet it is safe to say both words, with the responsibilities they carry, are God inspired and God approved; as are the more modern names for the ministry we find in churches today—greeter, door holder, amongst other names. While the ministry name may differ, the responsibilities almost mirror one another. Ushers can be found at church doors, typically welcoming members and guests; they assist with getting everyone seated, and also participate in the collection of offerings. This all sounds simple enough, like one of my favorite Geico Insurance commercials, "It's so easy a caveman can do it."

Such a view about church ushering will be a grossly erroneous one, however, that will lead any church into catastrophes beyond measure.

By way of background, I started ushering in 1986, when I was eighteen years old, at Ikoyi Baptist Church (IBC), Lagos, Nigeria. My journey into ushering remains memorable. IBC was my wife (who was my girlfriend at the time), Nike's church. She grew up at IBC, where she and her family were long-time members. After repeated requests from her to attend church services, I finally succumbed and summoned up the courage to walk in one Sunday. My main inhibition from attending in the first place is a symptom I call "Shy-nigitis," a made-up word I use to describe my extreme case of shyness (I think it could pass for a medical term, especially since it ends in "gitis" like a lot of medical conditions). I've always been a people person, but I always found groups of people or crowds unnerving, especially if they were people I didn't know.

After crossing the first hurdle, I actually made it through the church doors without fainting. Not only did I enjoy the service, which was Pentecostal in nature, with outstanding praise and worship consisting of a worship team and a regular choir, I realized I wanted more. Yours truly found himself becoming a regular attendee and then a member of the church. Unknown to me, the head usher at the time (initials A.J.) had taken a special interest in me and would allude to things about ushering being a role that requires many hands. I didn't quite understand what that had to do with me or why he was sharing all this with me at the time. To make a long story short, I think A.J. hypnotized me, because somehow I accepted his request to join the ushering ministry.

Me, with a strong case of Shy-nigitis! How did this happen? I know now the Lord had laid me on A.J.'s heart, that this was a ministry for me (as later affirmed by my pastor at the time, Reverend A.L., and several elders and deacons). Unknown to me, A.J., and I presume others, had been praying for me and working behind the scenes.

With both knees buckling and my heart in my mouth, I started ushering in both morning services and the evening service. What I found most shocking is the fact that from the very day I started, despite my nervousness, there was an absolute flow to everything I did. This is me, despite the large crowd that consisted of about 250 people for the first service and probably close to 400 for the second service. Hallelujah! God had healed me from Shy-nigitis, through circumstances I could never even dream of. I was soon voted in as the head usher of IBC, to the glory of God. All of this was happening so fast.

Know that God is able, abundantly able, to use you, and this is irrespective of anyone's opinion (including yours).

This experience remains a marked testimony for me. If God can use me in such an open way that I would have refused even if I was offered money for it, I am praying someone reading this will be encouraged and inspired to know that God has plans for your life and desires to use you as His partner in ministry, regardless of the things you see as flaws, inadequacies, or an irreparable past. Know that God is able, abundantly able, to use you, and this is irrespective of anyone's opinion (including yours). Know that the finished work of Jesus Christ on the cross of Calvary avails for you. Romans 4:25 lets us know that Jesus "was delivered over to death for our sins and was raised to life for our justification." Regardless of our past, current, or future state, we are justified through faith (Romans 5:1). By the mercy and grace of God, I remain an usher to date and currently serve as the head usher at Catalyst International Church (CIC) (formerly Catalyst Community Church) in Orlando, Florida.

One of the ministries ordained by God is the Ministry of Helps, as it is popularly called, but to be specific, it is a ministry of service, and I believe this is where the primary calling and ministry of an usher lies. It isn't enough to have good intentions and want to help out in the church. I firmly believe ushering is a calling that can't be fulfilled by everyone; the same way not everyone is called to be on the worship team (for obvious reasons) or any other ministry of the church. There must be a calling, as it pertains to the things of God, and as gifted by the Holy Spirit. 1 Corinthians 12:4-6 states that "There are different kinds of gifts, but the same Spirit distributes them. There are different kinds of service, but the same Lord. There are different kinds of working, but in all of them and in everyone it is the same God at work." This calling assures a covering from God and church leadership, starting with the pastor(s) of each church. 1 Corinthians 12:27-28 is instructive on the Ministry of Helps and other Ministries: "Now you are the body of Christ, and each one of you is a part of it. And God has placed in the church first of all apostles, second prophets, third teachers, then miracles, then gifts of healing, of helping, of guidance, and of different kinds of tongues." A study of this chapter reveals that no one ministry is more important than the other. To put this in blunt terms, God doesn't give brownie points to those who speak in tongues or to those who have the gift of healing over those who have the gift of teaching, or those who have the gift/ministry of helping.

The role of an usher, as with any other role in the church, should also not be based on any form of favoritism or personal preferences, when it comes to "recruiting" members to the ministry/team. This may sound like a case of the obvious, but the sad reality is that anomalies such as this exist in churches. God disapproves of favoritism:

My brothers and sisters, believers in our glorious Lord Jesus Christ must not show favoritism. Suppose a man comes into your meeting wearing a gold ring and fine clothes, and a poor man in filthy old clothes also comes in. If you show special attention to the man wearing fine clothes and say, "Here's a good seat for you," but say to the poor man, "You stand there" or "Sit on the floor by my feet," have you not discriminated among yourselves and become judges with evil thoughts? (James 2:1-4)

Interestingly enough, these verses are also relevant to the overall conduct of ushers; in terms of how they relate to every member and guest. I also believe that as the body of Christ, we are to distinguish ourselves from the way things are sometimes regrettably done in the circular or corporate world, where favoritism on various levels and for various reasons exist. It is common to hear of people deserving of promotions and pay raises being passed over or overlooked, not to mention someone doing all the work and someone else getting the credit. The difference we exhibit ought to be shown, not with a condescending attitude, implying superiority to others, but rather, one of humility and servanthood. We are to let our light shine (as we are encouraged to do from the Word of God) so that we make an impactful (positive) difference, such that we are attractive to those who are yet to receive Christ; in such a way that all we do cultivates an interest in them to want to know what makes us different. This is what I mean by distinguishing ourselves, that Christ may be glorified in and through us.

A general definition of the word usher from Merriam–Webster. com states the following:

a. An officer or servant who has the care of the door of a court, hall or chamber;

b. An officer who walks before a person of rank;

c. One who escorts persons to their seats (as in a theater).

Even from these definitions, there is a key consistency in an usher's role. An usher's role is that of a servant—one who serves. It isn't a position for the proud, those seeking to assert authority, delegate responsibilities, merely supervising and nothing else, or supposedly serving only to point out what is left undone or not done correctly by others. The heart of an usher must be the heart of a humble servant.

What greater example is there besides Jesus Christ Himself who said He did not come to be served, but to serve (Matthew 20:20-28; Mark 10:35-45). We also learn about what I consider to be the most profound example of humility (and submission) in Philippians 2:8, which lets us know that Jesus, being found in the appearance of man, humbled Himself by becoming obedient to death—even death on a cross. The essence of this remains unchanging. It was through His death that we receive the remission of our sins and our salvation. What a testimony! What a legacy Jesus left us to emulate and follow as His disciples.

As an usher, or anyone serving in the church in whatever capacity, anything short of the humility described in Philippians 2:1-8, misses the mark. To clarify, I am not asking that anyone invest in timber and commit a suicidal act on a cross. Jesus already paid the price for our salvation, once and for all! The death expected of each follower of Christ is death to self so that Christ is magnified. God's will then takes first place over our own will and way of doing things, and replaces our fleshly natural desires or tendencies with Holy Spirit inspired decisions and motivations. It will be a challenge to attempt creating an exhaustive list of responsibilities for ushers. I believe the role of an usher continues to evolve and some matters end up becoming an usher's responsibility to handle by default. Let's say Mrs. Witherspoon, for example, has a flat tire after the service. Everyone is eager to get to the restaurant for lunch or make the usual Sunday family visits (after church activities which ushers are also a part of). By default, I think the usual thought process would be to get an usher to change the tire, especially if Mrs. Witherspoon doesn't have AAA, or a similar service. I think this is reasonable, because a tire change should not involve having to call AAA that may end up taking over an hour for a process that can be handled in fifteen minutes (this is with the assumption, albeit an erroneous one, that all church ushers are capable of changing flat tires. It's my example and I'm sticking to it. You get the idea).

This is where a servant's heart and humility comes in. If you're saying or thinking, "Heck, no! It's not my role to change tires. Someone else needs to do that," there's a strong likelihood church ushering might not be right for you as a ministry to serve in. Of course, limitations due to physical constraints are understood. I often share a rhetorical question with my family by asking how as Christians we are to be the light to a lost and dying world if our light isn't shining among fellow brothers and sisters in Christ. If this extraordinary light of Christ is so dim among ourselves (by our actions or inactions, spiritual arrogance, selfishness, impatience, grumbling—please feel free to add to the list) that there is no visible evidence of its existence in us, then there's a monumental problem that calls for a rethink and self-examination of what being salt and light entails.

The next few chapters will attempt to cover specific roles I believe should be synonymous with church ushers and their role.

CHAPTER TWO

USHERS AS INTERCESSORS

There are no clearer terms I could use, other than to state that whenever there is a gathering of believers to fellowship, be it on a Sunday or midweek service, or any other occasion, principalities and powers, as described in the Bible, are at work, seeking to bring confusion, division, fear, and destruction to interrupt, and if possible, stop completely true fellowship among God's children. Ephesians 6:12 states "For we do not wrestle against flesh and blood, but against principalities, against powers, against the rulers of the darkness of this age, against spiritual hosts of wickedness in the heavenly places" (NKJV).

Sadly, for many, the existence of principalities, powers and contrary spirits is a subject they would rather avoid to the extent that they deny such forces exist. Breaking News…your denial does not change the unequivocal fact that they are real and are not just parts of scenes from a fictional horror movie. The Bible lets us know they exist. Something practically every Christian is guilty of at one point or the other is "cherry picking" the Word of God—we carefully select what is suitable for us, and overlook that which is uncomfortable or brings conviction. Yet while we feel validated (a self-validation) in doing this, it doesn't stop us from seeing the sin in others and pointing those sins out, sometimes not in love, but like the neighborhood spiritual vigilante. Of course the Bible encourages us to correct one another in love. Wake up! Accept it! Deal with it! Contrary spirits exist!

> *Wake up! Accept it! Deal with it! Contrary spirits exist!*

1 Peter 5:8 states "Be alert and of sober mind. Your enemy the devil prowls around like a roaring lion looking for someone to devour." Every time a "roaring lion" is mentioned in the Bible it relates to destruction. Judges 14:5, Psalm 22:13, Proverbs 28:15, Ezekiel 22:25, and Zephaniah 3:3 are instructive.

So what are these principalities and powers? Virtually everywhere one sees this phrase in the Bible, it relates to diabolical spirits that seek to contend against God's children. They are agents of satan who operate in the invisible realm with the mission of opposing and hindering God's children in every way possible. Even though they function in the invisible realm, they are able and very often use people they can influence, typically by possessing them, thus the reference to a person influenced by such contrary spirits as being possessed.

As a young usher at IBC, two incidents remain memorable and

noteworthy for this chapter. The first incident was during what was a normal morning service. Service had just started with the usual vibrant worship and praise, everyone on their feet, singing, and most people dancing as they could at their seats. I noticed a lady standing in the row ahead of me (I was stationed at a row reserved for ushers) turn slightly to the man to her left. Even though I could not see her face fully, it was apparent she was uncomfortable and scared.

Then I took a closer look at the man beside her and realized he had unbuttoned his shirt and was in the process of taking his shirt off right there, during service. (A quick brain scan brought to light that how to deal with people taking their clothes off during services was not in the usher's training manual.) Before he could take his shirt off completely, I took hurried but quiet steps toward him, gently put my arm around his shoulder, and asked quietly if he was okay. The instant my hand touched his shoulder, I felt an electric shock, like I just touched a live wire, all over my fingers. As you can imagine, I was petrified, in more ways than one. I was perturbed by what I just experienced and only God calmed me down so I didn't scream and thereby disrupt the service.

I immediately lifted my hand off his shoulder, but only very slightly so as not to make any contact to his body and so as not to create any swift motion that would draw the attention of others. I gently asked him to please put his shirt back on and button it up. At this point, because everyone was fully engaged in the worship and praise, I don't think too many people observed what just happened.

I went back to my seat, still in shock, literally with all my fingers tingling from the experience. I whispered to the other ushers what just happened, and they were all astonished and couldn't quite grasp what I had explained. It wasn't over; the same man started taking off his shirt again. At this point I was angry (a holy anger). I walked to him boldly, as God granted me the enabling, and firmly asked him to step outside to chat with me. He obliged.

I took him outside the door and stated assertively that we were in God's house and that he could not take off his shirt during service. I asked him why he was taking off his shirt. His response was that God told him to. I informed him that wasn't possible because God was not a God of confusion. I asked him if he could imagine God telling others in church to take their clothes off, what the service would look like. He chuckled and asked, "So it's not God?" And I said no, it cannot be God. While I was still talking with him, I noticed he was distracted and was looking into the church building, staring at the ceiling. I asked him what he was looking at. He responded, saying he was looking at those he came with…

Oh boy! At this point, I realized I couldn't just give him a stern warning and let him go back inside. I informed him that since I couldn't afford to have any further interruption to the service, he would have to sit in one of the overflow chairs outside the building (typically made available when the auditorium is full or when movement needs to be limited, notably when the sermon has started and to avoid unnecessary interruptions to the order or flow of service) where I could keep my eyes on him. Thankfully, that worked and the rest of the service went uninterrupted. All of this happened so fast that decisions had to be made instantaneously, with no opportunity to confer with anyone.

With the usual exchanging of pleasantries after the service, I couldn't get a hold of any of the pastors to inform them of what I had just experienced, but I got the opportunity when I went back for the evening service. I saw our Assistant Pastor and Music Minister, Pastor E.A., and informed him of what transpired in the morning. What further shocked me is the fact that just as I informed him I put my arm on the man's shoulder, and before I could complete my sentence, he laughed and said, "You got an electric shock, right?"

My mouth was wide open from the surprise of hearing that he knew what happened. I asked how he knew that. He laughed again and said don't worry about it and reassured me that I would be fine, stating that the contrary spirit at work in the man, was a "spirit of confusion" that wasn't purposed to cause physical harm, but rather, an interruption of the service in any way possible. The contrary spirit was there to take away from the orderly flow of the service, the reverence and the anointing. He couldn't stop laughing and then congratulated me, saying I've now been officially inducted into what ministry entails. Oh, I forgot to mention Pastor E.A. was also in charge of the deliverance ministry, so he was very familiar with contrary/demonic spirits!

This experience necessitated changes to how we ushered as a whole. There was the need for increased vigilance, both in the natural and spiritual, through fervent prayers and intercession. It was obvious we all needed to pay closer attention to all activity and movements during services, no matter how routine or ordinary they looked. There was a better awareness of the need to not only cover the services in prayer, but ourselves as well, as we served.

The second incident brought about a different dimension to how we pray during any prayer time. It was almost the end of service this Sunday morning at IBC and at the end of the message, a prayer of reflection was being made by the Pastor (A.L.). As was the practice, all heads were bowed and all eyes were closed…everyone reverencing the moment, as is typically said. With my eyes closed, I heard what sounded like a quiet scuffle, if that makes any sense. All I knew was that the sound I heard didn't sound like one of reverence. I looked up and I noticed one of the Deacons (Deacon O., who usually sits upfront, close to the pulpit) carrying a woman from the pulpit on his shoulder with his hand over her mouth, hurriedly down the stairs of the pulpit and straight outside.

What just happened? I noticed the pastor kept an eye on what was going on, but kept on praying and concluded the service calmly. Of course, as soon as service ended, I made inquiries about what happened. Turns out the pastor's prayer struck a nerve with this woman who was possessed and in a fit of rage, charged toward the Pastor, lunging at his throat, in an attempt to strangle him. Thanks to Deacon O., the situation was averted, our Pastor lived and it was a happy ending.

This required another meeting with the ushers to review how we function. I came up with the decision that we were all to keep our eyes open during prayer times. While our heads may be bowed, we need to maintain a visual of the entire auditorium, watching for any unusual or sudden movement that otherwise should not occur during a prayer time.

One particular incident stands out at CIC. I thank God for a church that truly exemplifies God's love—agape love. As is the slogan with the local PF Gym, CIC is "a judgment free zone." All are welcome and all receive the same loving genuine welcome. Over a decade ago, a lady started attending with her two teenage sons. She seemed troubled, with a lot on her mind. She would cry loudly (more of wailing/shrieks) during services and in the usual loving fashion, other women in the service would gather around her, comfort her, hug her, and pray with her.

Over time, the wailing intensified into extremely loud and distracting sounds that would overpower Pastor D.M.'s preaching. I am aware Pastor D.M. made efforts to counsel this lady and minister to her in every way possible, but it appeared the more she got attention, the more she pushed the boundary. Her wailing now moved from the aisles to the front of the pulpit where she would fall to the ground and wail in the most unimaginable way, refusing any comforting. It became obvious to many there was more to this than the ordinary course of things. Contrary spirits were there at work, disrupting services, to the extent that some members left services because of the overpowering shrieking. A decision was made that another meeting had to take place with this lady, but before that could happen, she had yet another wailing takeover as the devotional during a Wednesday service was about to be shared.

She was seated on a side aisle, close to an exit/kitchen door. I quietly walked to her, as inconspicuously as I could and gently asked her to please note that service could not proceed after the opening prayer because of the distraction from all the screaming. She told me my statement came from the devil, and before I could fully respond, one of her teenage sons seated behind her grabbed me close to my neck and told me his mom could do whatever she wanted and to leave her alone. It all happened in a flash. I had to get his grip off my neck, and all I remember is somehow (quietly) moving myself with her son into the exit/kitchen door, where I was able to shake him off (this is a summarized version I'm giving). Pastor D.M. was close behind me and ordered them out, informing them they were no longer welcome at the church. It had become very apparent this woman was not willing to submit to authority in the church, and had clearly acted in ways that discouraged some members from coming to church. The intent and spirit at work in this woman was clear—disrupt and take over every service, and she was succeeding.

That was the last we saw of her and her sons, but again, there was the need to revisit the drawing board to review situations such as this in a bid to prevent, or at best minimize them. The women of the church who were gifted in spiritual warfare were given the authorization from leadership to address cases such as this (involving women) when it was clear contrary spirits were at work. The acts of this woman single handedly interfered with the order of services, the anointing, and distracted many from focusing on the messages. There was a further realization, that in addition to prayer and spiritual warfare, which are of the utmost importance, there are times when further action is required, such as the need to have disruptive people removed from services, and with the assistance of law enforcement, if necessary.

Why have I shared these experiences? To shed light on the truth of God's Word in Ephesians 6:12 cited above. As ushers, one must start each service (and each day) in fervent prayer, interceding for the pastors of the church, the service, other members, and the various ministries. Simply put, the whole service has to be committed to God's hands, and importantly, praying for one another. As led by the Spirit, what has been set in place at CIC is a prayer time amongst the ushers before each service starts. We also have an intercessory team in place, with members praying before and during services.

We cannot rely on how long we've been ushering, how familiar we are with the members of the church, or how small or large the church is. The Word of God is clear, "'Not by might nor by power, but by my Spirit,' says the Lord Almighty" (Zechariah 4:6). Complete dependence and submission to the Holy Spirit will open eyes to more than the ordinary course of things, or the "business as usual" attitude or complacency that sometimes comes from the monotony associated with ushering.

CHAPTER THREE

USHERS AS PEACEMAKERS

It's usual to hear me say jokingly during services that there's never a dull moment. The truth of the matter is that no two services are the same. Regardless of planning and preparation, an occurrence that requires quick thinking or spontaneous adjustments is common. While not every situation involves tense matters, in general and for an usher especially, it is of the utmost importance to ensure our actions do not **escalate** a tense situation, but rather, provides a **remedy** for it. People come to church with emotions at work. Some are angry, maybe from an argument with a loved one before leaving for church. Some overwhelmed by a challenging situation that lingers, and these are two among so many other scenarios. Might I add that included in those with these emotions are the very ushers themselves. We have to humbly pray for God to clothe and immerse us with His holiness to function in a way that will be pleasing and acceptable to Him during services, and quite frankly, at all times.

Picture a first-time guest, a mother who walks in with a baby. Before long, the cute baby is perhaps hungry, hot, cold, or irritable for some reason. It's usually hard to pinpoint which it is with babies. Either way, scene two commences...the baby starts crying and all eyes in the auditorium are on the poor mother who is flustered already and trying to calm down. Some eyes are looks of compassion, others, I must admit, are looks of annoyance. You can almost imagine movie projectors from the foreheads of some members displaying the words that capture what's on their minds; "Get that baby out of here!"

Now here's where the usher comes in, to request that mom take her adorable baby out of the main auditorium, to a nursery, even though she made it clear when she first came in that she didn't feel comfortable leaving her baby there, more so since it was her first time at the church. This is a valid concern in my opinion, but nevertheless, the service, especially the sermon must continue without interruption, especially those that can be addressed, or avoided.

I firmly believe we can speak powerfully if we allow the Holy Spirit to do the talking.

So how does one convince this mother who is already feeling pressure from the movie projectors on the foreheads of half of the congregation? I firmly believe we can speak powerfully if we allow the Holy Spirit to do the talking. At CIC, I have been assigned with the sole responsibility of addressing scenarios such as the one described above. In line with all I shared in the previous chapter, I approach mothers in this situation prayerfully, and this is not meant to be a holy cliché. I ask God to speak through me before I approach the mother(s); I approach them gently, get on one knee in front of them, so they don't feel like the spotlight is on them (even though it already is) and softly inform them we have a beautiful nursery where the babies can play with fun toys and maybe get to make a new friend. I encourage the mother to stay in the nursery with her baby if that will make her feel more comfortable, since the nursery is at the back of the auditorium, with tinted windows and speakers, allowing the mother to still be a part of the service, as they are able to hear the message. If there's the need for added persuasion, my wild card is to tell them the nursery is my favorite place to hang out when my wife, Nike, puts me on time out.

This may seem comical, but with all seriousness, what has always happened, by the mercy and grace of God, is that a tense situation is remedied. It gives me indescribable joy when after the brief conversation, some of the mothers even hand me the baby to take to the nursery myself. I share this to make a crucial point: **exerting or showing that you have authority does not always mean that authority will be acknowledged or respected**. Let your authority flow from a standpoint of love and humility. Then your authority speaks for itself and will be acknowledged and respected. It's vital to function as a person with compassion and not like a robot that's just programmed to follow a blueprint. I personally feel using a stern voice with the mother(s) and ordering them to take the baby out, may accomplish getting the baby out, but it may be with the mother taking the baby out, feeling disrespected and embarrassed, vowing never to return to the church, or she may simply walk out of the church with the same vow.

I realize not all churches are the same in terms of how they operate; the order of services; the structure of the buildings, and how matters of contention are handled. However, a peaceful and loving approach is always advisable. A life-changing statement I will always remember was made by one of my former Pastors (Pastor D.M.) while I was seated in his office. I was upset on his behalf because I felt he was being taken advantage of by a former member. This member had left the church without notice and returned years later asking him to conduct her wedding ceremony, to which he agreed. I expressed how upset I was at the audacity of this lady, compounded by the fact that she came to him as a last resort.

He smiled and very calmly (his trademark demeanor) told me he felt exactly how I felt, and then said, "But remember, Lanre, the goal is always to win the brother or sister over." That one statement positively impacted my life in more ways than I can describe. If by exerting authority you hurt or discourage people, what mark have you left? It's highly unlikely the hurt mother with the crying baby will have a good report to share about the church. This is not to say there won't be situations when you've done all you know to do and the mother still ends up leaving upset. But before God and man, you want to have the assurance that you did all you could do in love. 1 Corinthians 13 is insightful and relevant. This is the same in any ministry and position in church, from the pastor to servants in all ministries. Servants of God should continually seek and encourage a mindset that purposes, "to win the brother or sister over."

Other situations may arise where the peace-making process requires nothing but silence. In other words, no response at all. The Bible says, "A gentle answer turns away wrath, but a harsh word stirs up anger" (Proverbs 15:1). Just because you can say something or have the authority to say it, doesn't necessarily make it right to say it, more so in terms of how it's expressed. No one appreciates being spoken to in a demeaning or condescending way. Not only is this kind of speech rude, it's ungodly and won't reflect the light of Christ in us. Sometimes the tense situation arises not from something that was said, but by your response to what was said. Crying out for the Holy Spirit's help is indispensable, to know when to speak, and when to be silent.

A case in point occurred many years ago, during former president Barack Obama's first election. CIC is used as one of the voting centers, and as is our practice, the overall experience of everyone that comes to our location is paramount. We strive to ensure everyone is welcomed, feels welcomed and loved, whether or not the occasion is a church related program. Clearly, having voting machines set up all over the church auditorium cannot be considered to be a church program, but still we had lots of members volunteering their time to hand out water to anyone in need, to answer questions, and assist with the parking and safety of vehicles.

As can be imagined, being a landmark presidential election, there was a constant flow of vehicles coming in and out of the church, with an overflow of cars onto our adjoining property, which was a field. This is where I was located, ensuring vehicles were properly spaced, so no one was blocked in and also to ensure no vehicle blocked the pathway meant for entries and exits. A vehicle pulled up in front of me and I waved my hand to say hello and get her attention, then guided her to the next available spot on the field. After parking, she came out of her vehicle and when she was close enough, I said "Good evening, ma'am, welcome." Nothing prepared me for the response I received.

"You want to know what's a problem?" She said, "This church that can't provide parking." After hurriedly getting over her shocking response, I very gently said, "I'm sorry about that, ma'am," and clearly heard the Holy Spirit instruct me to say no more, so I obeyed and gently motioned her toward the direction of the church entrance. This lady appeared to have already been in a rage before she drove into the church, and I really felt deep inside me that anything I said beyond the apology, no matter how well intended, would have escalated the situation.

With all this being said, it is unrealistic not to expect situations that will test the patience of an usher or make an usher upset during services, and this I have seen happen. What I recommend in such situations is for the usher to walk away from it politely, report it to the head usher or to anyone else in leadership as is appropriate and have another usher handle the matter, to avoid tempers flaring. Not only does this put a different and calm usher into the matter, it also provides the upset usher with the time to calm down, and if need be, refrain from ushering for the rest of the service. Here's another news flash…ushers have emotions too; they may have had an argument with a spouse, child, or other family member before service, just like you; or maybe didn't get enough sleep the night before. Bottom line, it doesn't hurt for the member that has the expectation of being pampered twenty-four seven to realize the ushers could do with a bit of pampering too, even if all it entails is expressing appreciation for all they do. I encourage all ushers to provide feedback and communicate any concerns or issues that may arise during any service. This is one of the ways we're able to improve and make necessary adjustments.

Ushers' feedback and communication further stresses the undeniable need for fervent prayer at all times. We are encouraged in 1 Thessalonians 5:17 to pray continually (NIV). The King James Version states that we should pray without ceasing. It is foolhardy to attempt doing anything, even if it seems mundane, without being Spirit filled. It is crucial to ask the Holy Spirit to work in and through you. This prayer and submission to God's guidance though the Holy Spirit works wonders, and I mean that literally. He (the Holy Spirit) will give you revelation concerning things and place in your mouth words that are not yours, but inspired by Him, and this will always make a difference between harmony and chaos in the Church.

CHAPTER FOUR

USHERS AS WATCHMEN

There is no doubt that the current state of affairs worldwide makes it indispensable for an usher's role to include the overall safety and well-being of not only members and guests alike, but also the safety of church property. For a countless number, the church was always a safe haven, where you could let your guard down, so to speak. Focus during services and other church programs wasn't hindered by distractions such as worrying whether or not an intruder would barge in with a gun intent on murdering members for absolutely no justifiable reason. Unfortunate and repeated occurrences of churches and other places of worship being invaded by gunmen who senselessly kill innocent and unarmed individuals is an all too familiar story in recent times.

Churches and other places of worship now find themselves faced with difficult decisions concerning how to protect their members and buildings from such attacks. This is easier said than done because some of the decisions to be made are uncomfortable ones. The sad reality is regardless of how uncomfortable these decisions may be, they must be made as part of an evolving process in the day to day functionality of a church, and other places of worship.

Churches and other places of worship are also not exempt from theft, both externally and internally. There are cases of burglaries when these buildings are unoccupied and there are cases of theft even during services—purses are stolen, for example, and cars are broken into. Part of ushering protocol may necessitate patrolling the parking lot periodically. This could be done in turns, between ushers or through the use of a schedule, so no single usher is inundated with the task of being solely responsible for the "Parking Lot Duty."

While on this point, it is important for me to state that my keen observation after all these years of ushering is that most ushers will not decline a role, especially if that role request comes from the pastor. Sadly, rather than that usher speaking up and explaining that he has gotten more than his fair share of a sun tan from being constantly outside throughout the duration of every service, not to mention the crucial fact that such an usher is not being spiritually fed, since they never hear the message, such an usher or volunteer simply stops coming to church at some point. When called to inquire about their well-being, they still refrain from saying how they feel, and give convenient excuses or reasons why they no longer attend church.

Typically, the word gets out soon thereafter that they're attending another church with their family. Such an usher or volunteer cannot be deemed to have backslidden, as one will typically hear, whenever a member leaves a church. The point is thoughtful and sensitive consideration must be given to assigning roles, so no one gets overwhelmed or feels taken for granted. If in a bid to be of service to the church, an usher or volunteer is not being spiritually fed or has become worn out, especially when there should be a clear and reasonable expectation that this is likely, bearing in mind the magnitude of assigned tasks, then the purpose of being in church for such an individual is defeated.

So where does the usher come in? Because of the level of involvement of ushers in church programs the matter of security is intertwined. There are churches that have a separate volunteer security team, which sometimes requires the aid of police officers to be present during services, or the engagement of security companies. But regardless, there must be some coordination with ushers, who are sometimes part of the security team. Some of the uncomfortable decisions to be made include whether or not to have members armed. I for one struggled with this idea, but over time have come to terms with the fact that there is wisdom in such a decision. The intent is not to be the aggressor, but rather to quell a situation that could otherwise result in the loss of multiple lives. This is such a delicate matter that it requires careful deliberations and training to ensure that decisions are not made irrationally, out of fear, bias, stereotype, or otherwise prematurely and unjustifiably.

As an initial step, all ushers should be prayerfully vigilant. No watchman should be found distracted, uninterested, or slothful in action. A watchman's role is a huge responsibility as can be found from numerous verses in the Bible. Noteworthy is Ezekiel 33:1-6:

The word of the Lord came to me: "Son of man, speak to your people and say to them: 'When I bring the sword against a land, and the people of the land choose one of their men and make him their watchman, and he sees the sword coming against the land and blows the trumpet to warn the people, then if anyone hears the trumpet but does not heed the warning and the sword comes and takes their life, their blood will be on their own head. Since they heard the sound of the trumpet but did not heed the warning, their blood will be on their own head. If they had heeded the warning, they would have saved themselves. But if the watchman sees the sword coming and does not blow the trumpet to warn the people and the sword comes and takes someone's life, that person's life will be taken because of their sin, but I will hold the watchman accountable for their blood.'"

> *No watchman should be found distracted, uninterested, or slothful in action.*

It is vital for ushers to be familiar with the surroundings of the church, both indoors and outdoors. A clear understanding of all entry/exit points is essential; fire extinguishers must be checked periodically to make sure they are up to date; they must be aware of where first aid kits are; it is helpful to involve someone in the medical field or a paramedic as part of the ushering team; church lighting, indoors and outdoors, should be noted for functionality;

the landscaping should be assessed for overgrown tree branches where an intruder could hide; assessing all doors to ensure they lock properly; observing unusual body language that may be a sign of danger or of someone in distress are some of the matters to be addressed. While some matters may not necessarily be the responsibility of ushers (such as landscaping), it is beneficial to be aware of such concerns so they can be reported appropriately.

Ushers need to be strategically positioned during services. Besides the obvious case of ensuring members and guests alike are promptly seated, being properly spread out within the auditorium creates the ability to observe every part of the auditorium for what may seem like unusual or odd activities. It is important for the head usher of the church to maintain the same position during services, preferably at the main door to the auditorium/main sanctuary (this is a suggestion from what has worked effectively at IBC and CIC). This way he or she is able to get a peripheral view of the service and make eye contact with all other ushers regarding not only the availability of seats, but also regarding any other concern.

The issue of guns inside churches clearly has to be addressed separately and subjectively. In the event that a decision is made to authorize this, it cannot be overemphasized that all gun carriers have to be properly licensed to do so. State and federal laws must be examined to ensure compliance. Part of the training and evaluation should include an assessment of the mental and psychological state of all gun carriers. As hard as it is to say this, it is disheartening that there are trigger happy folks out there who would jump at the opportunity to be a part of such a team, simply because the opportunity now exists to bring to reality all that has been practiced at the gun range. This is not a random statement. On January 31, 2018, I attended a "Safety and Security In Your Place of Worship" summit for places of worship, organized by the Orange County Sheriff's Office in Orlando, Florida.

During one of the segments on crime prevention, real life examples were given on when not to use a firearm. One example remains entrenched in my mind, especially from the video shown, used to replicate what transpired. A church service had just started; some members already seated, and others were entering. A man walks in and sits on the first chair in an aisle on the extreme left side of the church, toward the middle row. As he sits down, a man behind him gently taps him on the shoulder and quietly informs him the seat he's on was taken (nothing was on the seat to indicate it was taken or occupied by someone else). The man who just sat down turns around instantly and hits off the hand of the man behind him off his shoulder, telling him to leave him alone. An usher close by hurriedly walks to the man who just sat down and introduces himself as an usher in an abrasive way, grabbing the man by the arm. The man gets up and punches the usher in the face. The usher reaches for his concealed gun and proceeds to shoot the man in the chest. The man dies, and of course it's highly unlikely church service was able to resume thereafter. A life was lost all because a seat had apparently been reserved and someone else sat in it.

What gave me goosebumps was a statement uttered by someone

beside me who said in his opinion, the use of force with a gun in the incident just described was justified as a case of self-defense, totally defeating the purpose behind that segment of the seminar; which was to emphasize the fact that just because firearms are available, that doesn't make it right to use them at any opportunity that arises. Who knows what state of mind the deceased was in? Was he mentally unstable; upset from a prior occurrence and wanting to find succor at a church? No one will ever know, because of an overzealous trigger-happy usher who would face murder charges.

It was repeatedly stated during this segment: "Always remember, it's your gun, it's your bullet." Bottom line, once the trigger is pulled, it will warrant an investigation to determine whether or not the use of the firearm was justified. The house of God now becomes a potential crime scene; local TV stations are on board to get their fair share of everyone's opinion, with scenes of the church periodically aired on TV; the pastor has to look for biblical ways to appease and assure the congregants and public at large that all is well; there are potential law suits…you get the picture.

Ushers, with grace, may be able to deescalate a situation, through their demeanor, speech, and voice tone rather than aggravate it. There will be instances where a firearm may be required purely in self-defense and to protect the lives of members at risk from being shot and potentially killed, but as a first resort, my position remains to call out to God in prayer ceaselessly, for protection at all times and to rely on Him and seek Him as the ultimate protector, rather than place first reliance on the fact that guns are available for use.

Such reliance could create distractions and a lack of focus, taking away from the due recognition of God's sovereign power and ability to protect and shield us.

The same God who protected Daniel in the lion's den and Shadrach, Meshach, and Abednego from flames of fire is able to protect us from gun attacks too. This is by no means implying that the unfortunate victims of gun violence in places of worship did not pray for protection in the first place, or in the past, but rather, an admonition not to put God in second place when it comes to protection.

There may be less severe cases (where guns aren't involved) that may pertain to a heated argument between two or more church members (yes, I have seen this happen too); the tumultuous situation does not have to be from an outsider or an intruder. It is vital for ushers to stay watchful and not allow emotions get the better of them, especially if the argument involves a member they have a close relationship with. Objectivity and an unbiased approach must be the preferred way of diffusing the situation. Shouting when those arguing are already shouting will only worsen the situation. It will be best for female ushers if possible to separate females confronting each other. This lessens the likelihood of claims or allegations of inappropriate contact being made by an usher.

So many factors need to be considered before making any decision, as churches aren't immune from lawsuits either. Let's not forget that the enemy of our souls only seeks to kill, steal, and destroy in any way possible and will stop at nothing to accomplish this, but God fights for us, as our Protector and Defender!

Jesus Himself instructed us to "Be always on the watch, and pray that you may be able to escape all that is about to happen, and that you may be able to stand before the Son of Man " (Luke 21:36).

CHAPTER FIVE

USHERS AS FACILITATORS

Whether or not ushers realize it, they play an indispensable role in ensuring an atmosphere of holy reverence, prior, during, and after services and in all church activities. There are many details in church activities that end up not necessarily being taken for granted, but perhaps automatically expected to happen. In reality, a myriad of details and logistical matters go into any church activity that ushers typically facilitate.

I'll use an example to illustrate what hopefully everyone can relate to. We all expect our trash, which we put outside to be picked up by a trash company or by the county, whichever the case may be, to be disposed of by workers who go around each neighborhood. Oftentimes, the general impression one gets is that it's their job—they're paid to do it, and as such there doesn't appear to be appreciation for what they do. Let's picture a scenario where the workers for the company responsible for picking up and disposing of your trash make a decision to go on strike, to protest unfavorable working conditions (perhaps the lack of suitable gloves or masks to perform their duties, or an increase in salary).

The implication of this strike is that your garbage remains uncollected. A survey will show that most people will have sentiments of anger and disgust that their trash has not been picked up. Unbearable odors ooze from place to place, and the majority don't stop to think that these workers (all of whom I have tremendous respect for) have every right to go on strike too, just like any other worker, such as those at Disney World and SeaWorld who go on strike now and again to complain about unfavorable conditions or salaries. The expectation is that our trash has to be picked up by some random man or woman, without appreciation for the value of what they do, until what they do is taken away.

Coming back to ushers, their role is vital in ensuring the overall smooth flow of each service and all programs. There must be a symphony, as in a musical composition that moves through every aspect of the service. For example, an interruption for whatever reason in one of the children's classrooms could disrupt the entire service. Such an interruption has to be promptly addressed. As repeatedly stated, the adversary of our souls is extremely sly and in carrying out responsibilities, ushers have to be vigilant and watchful to ensure that nothing in our actions or conduct ends up being a distraction either—our voice tone, when we talk, does it seem harsh, irritated, or condescending? How we are dressed (our overall appearance), is it befitting for a church service? In the introductory paragraph, I mentioned that a specific dress code isn't necessarily a mandate for ushers or for ushering, as can be seen from various churches. I however believe it should be presentable and respectable. Ushers and everyone else in ministry must ensure that how they are dressed is befitting, appropriate, and not in any way capable of causing distractions. I believe with the Holy Spirit at work in us, we can look at ourselves in the mirror every Sunday morning (and on other occasions) and clearly hear the Holy Spirit speak, saying to a lady, that dress is too short or revealing. To a man, maybe that shirt needs to be ironed, or those shoes need to be polished. The intent is not to dress to impress anyone (that mindset is also a distraction that the devil can take advantage of). Rather, we should strive to represent ourselves well, as individuals, such that we let the light of Christ shine through us, even with the way we dress. By so doing, we also represent our church well, and the office we hold. At CIC, our ushers do an outstanding job in terms of all they do, and maintain a decent and respectable dress code. The beauty there (CIC), as previously mentioned, is that it is a judgement free zone, where the pettiness and distraction that comes from focusing on what others are wearing does not exist (we do require that everyone wear something though).

As part of the usher's manual, which I provide to every usher and potential usher, is a recommendation to carry breath mints in their pockets, to be enjoyed at intervals, but specifically before services start and at the end of services. This is when we tend to interact with people the most. Let's face it, we all have bad breath at one point or the other. It's a natural occurrence and really should not be seen as a case of lack of personal hygiene. It could be from that sandwich you enjoy with onions or garlic in it, like I do; from coffee, or simply from a dry mouth. But in a bid to be facilitators of services, we also don't want bad breath to hinder the service for anyone, by it being a distraction. If that is all someone thinks about after interacting with one of us…yikes! While we continue to be breath-mint patrons at CIC and for other churches that are encouraged to adopt this after reading this book, I will include a playful disclaimer here that while our breath-mint intake may not be 100 percent proof, I ask that ushers participating be given 100 percent for effort and thoughtfulness in this regard.

Examples where facilitating a smooth order of service is crucial will include instances where not only does a cell phone ring during service, but the individual who owns the phone decides to engage in a conversation right there during service (Yes, it's happened…no church specified, in case you're wondering). The phone ringing in the first place is already a distraction. That can't be changed, but the situation involving the conversation thereafter must be addressed promptly and tactfully.

One of the many things I've learned through law school and law practice in general is that you cannot and should not make assumptions, no matter how clear the case or the circumstance may seem. There is always an indispensable need to unravel all the facts and not to make a decision or conclusion, based on limited facts you either know, witnessed, personal bias, stereotype, past bad experiences, or simply by the circumstances at hand. Why am I giving this tutorial? Because the immediate human reaction is typically to feel disappointment by the fact that someone is actually having a conversation in church during a service. But could it be that this call was related to an emergency from someone the individual who received the call was shocked to hear from, and could not compose himself or herself enough to get up and leave before answering the phone? Could the individual be in so much shock from the information received that he or she totally lost awareness momentarily as to where they were and trying

The cogent point here is how the matter is handled. At all times, it must be in love and with respect.

to mentally process the information just received? Of course I'm giving hypothetical scenarios as food for thought. The reality is we, as ushers, don't know and neither does the rest of the congregation already making conclusions in situations such as those just described. The cogent point here is how the matter is handled. At all times, it must be in love and with respect.

My approach, which I encourage all ushers to adopt, is to quietly sit beside the individual if there is room to do so, or kneel/squat in front of them (if no physical limitation precludes you from doing so) and quietly ask the individual if everything is okay and then gently ask if he or she could kindly continue with the conversation in the lobby, or in any event, outside the auditorium/sanctuary. Another option is to gently put your arm around the individual's shoulder if you are unable to get in front of them and whisper the same inquiry and request close to their ear (this is another area where those breath mints come in handy). This approach also deescalates any tension the individual may be feeling. The Bible encourages us to strive to do everything in love (1 Corinthians 16:14). Your authority will be respected and appreciated if it is carried out in love, and not forcefully or in a controlling manner.

CHAPTER SIX

USHERS AS PEOPLE OF INTEGRITY

I will always consider ushers to be servants, to the glory of God, fulfilling noble responsibilities for the kingdom of God. Anything done for God's kingdom should be seen as service unto the Lord. Regrettably, because of modern day titles, many see their positions or offices in church as strictly one of authority, rather than of servant-hood. With authority only in mind, and the quest to exert that authority, focus is lost or taken away from the true essence of why you exist and function in that position or office. The true essence of any office or position is to be used as a yielded vessel of God; to bring glory to His name and to facilitate all that will help spread the Good News.

It goes without saying that Pastors alone can't do it all. For a church to thrive, stay healthy, and grow, it takes teams of ministries to keep the banner of Christ flying. It was for this reason that the twelve apostles selected helpers from within the disciples to help in facilitating the work of the Ministry (Acts 6:1-7). Help was needed, but there was a standard required for those who would be helpers.

In Acts 6:3, the men to be chosen were to be those known to be full of the Spirit and wisdom.

Help was needed, but there was a standard required for those who would be helpers.

By the same token, 1 Timothy 3:1-13 states the qualifications for overseers and deacons:

"Here is a trustworthy saying: Whoever aspires to be an overseer desires a noble task. Now the overseer is to be above reproach, faithful to his wife, temperate, self-controlled, respectable, hospitable, able to teach, not given to drunkenness, not violent but gentle, not quarrelsome, not a lover of money. He must manage his own family well and see that his children obey him, and he must do so in a manner worthy of full respect. (If anyone does not know how to manage his own family, how can he take care of God's church?) He must not be a recent convert, or he may become conceited and fall under the same judgment as the devil. He must also have a good reputation with outsiders, so that he will not fall into disgrace and into the devil's trap. In the same way, deacons are to be worthy of respect, sincere, not indulging in much wine, and not pursuing dishonest gain. They must keep hold of the deep truths of the faith with a clear conscience. They must first be tested; and then if there is nothing against them, let them serve as deacons. In the same way, the women are to be worthy of respect, not malicious talkers but temperate and trustworthy in everything. A deacon must be faithful to his wife and must manage his children and his household well. Those who have served well gain an excellent standing and great assurance in their faith in Christ Jesus."

Regardless of the title, all who serve in every true church of the Living God is a servant. Ushers, as servants, I believe are subject to the same standards stated above. We are firsthand representatives of the church. Our conduct and how matters are handled are a reflection of the church, as already mentioned. How Jesus Christ's love permeated everything He did suffices to cover any example I could possibly give, in terms of how things should be done. **This love, primarily, and the necessary training in terms of protocol and order, will be of tremendous benefit to all churches in terms of how the ushering ministry (and all other ministries) function.**

With all this being said, I am mindful that even with your best effort undertaken in love, there will be people who cannot be pleased. There are those who are too inwardly focused on themselves that, regardless of what you do, it's just never enough. Their individual need surpasses that of everyone else. The standard I believe should be to do everything with the power of the Holy Spirit at work in you, regardless of any hurt you feel through the bad conduct or attitude of any member, such that if any charge or false accusation is brought against you, no fault will be found (Daniel 6:4).

Continue to do your part in love and let God Himself fight/speak for you. I know this can be easier said than done, but in the long run, I have found that this approach remains the best approach.

For instance, a constant Sunday morning challenge involves body temperature. Allow me to explain before your imagination runs too wild. It is common to have several approach me and say, "It's too hot in here," and another faction saying "It's too cold in here." How does one please both sides? Talk about needing the wisdom of Solomon.

Initially I tried regulating the thermostats, but this never made a difference, as the complaints continued from one of the factions. Again, in this case, there had to be a standard, so after agonizing in prayer (I mean that) all air-conditioning units had to be set at a uniform and reasonable level, and my response to each side thereafter was "I'm so sorry about that. We have tried to set the thermostats to a temperature we feel will be comfortable for everyone." Not everyone who heard this was necessarily convinced or impressed by my response, notably by the visible muttering as they walked away, dissatisfied they didn't get their way; but as I often share with the ushering team, certain sensitive situations come with the job description and can't be avoided. In the situation described, we certainly can't have everyone getting up and adjusting the thermostats themselves and as they please.

This book would be tainted with falsehood if I didn't state that there are times as an usher, when your integrity will be called into question. The last thing I want to do is to paint a picture of perfection, such that the impression I'm giving is that once you've prayed, reviewed the training manual, and of course, indulged in the breath mints, all will be well. Far from it! Let's draw our attention to the point already stated that the enemy of our souls comes only to kill, steal, and destroy. These words should not be taken lightly, or just glossed over when you read verses concerning this, or hear messages involving this. Any attempt to kill, steal, or destroy anything concerning your life, including your family and ministry, is in complete opposition to God's plans for you. There are two completely opposite ends we have to prayerfully fight to ensure they never meet, in Jesus name.

God's plan: "plans to prosper you and not to harm you, plans to give you hope and a future" (Jeremiah 29:11).

The devil's plan: "to kill and steal and destroy" (John 10:10).

The reality we are oftentimes oblivious to is that the devil seeks to bring destruction to us in any and every way possible. In a big way or in a small way, he'll take what he can get; no fair game, no cards are off the table. So if he can kill you emotionally, financially, relationally, and thereby create a spirit of offense or unforgiveness, he'll do that without necessarily focusing on your literal physical death, although he'll attempt that too. The same goes for how he seeks to steal and destroy; it's in every way possible. One of the tools used by the devil in attempts to carry out his schemes is to bring confusion howsoever. This has been previously mentioned. But confusion how? Again, I'll reiterate, confusion in every way possible. This will include specifically and for purposes of this chapter on integrity, confusion through attempts to kill, steal, and destroy your reputation or character by bringing accusations, notably false, misconceived or preconceived accusations, based on limited or distorted facts.

If there are accusations, the Bible lets us know that the devil is the accuser of the brethren (Revelation 12:10). Prayer remains the key; our secret weapon for all spiritual warfare. My encouragement to anyone in the ushering ministry (or any other ministry) faced with unjustified accusations is to refrain from angry and hurried reactions. There are things that will sometimes cause us to be angry. I salute those who say they are never angry, because there is clarity in the Bible that shows that there are times anger will arise, but the Bible also instructs us not to let our anger cause us to sin (Daniel 4:26). The NIV version says "In your anger do not sin." The NLT version says "don't sin by letting your anger control you." The ESV version says "Be angry and do not sin." Your anger may be justified, but do not let it cause you to sin and allow the enemy to create other divisive occurrences beyond that which is at hand. Pray a prayer of vindication! It works! God will grant you His peace as the matter remains in abeyance.

CHAPTER SEVEN

USHERS AS AMBASSADORS OF THE CHURCH

Repeatedly, I have stated that ushers, for the most part are the first point of contact for church members and guests alike. I also can't overemphasize the importance and the truth to the fact that this first interaction with anyone who comes into a church can be a "make or break" experience— the individual(s) either feels a warm and welcoming experience that serves as encouragement to come back to the church, or the experience could leave the individual feeling mistreated, unwelcome, and otherwise disappointed, resulting in no desire to return. Either experience has consequences that will either enhance growth in the church or discourage growth, more so because in my opinion (for what it's worth) word of mouth feedback will always be the most effective form of advertising.

An individual's experience at a church service or event, more specifically, interactions with ushers don't end there. That experience carries over beyond the church service or event. Let's envisage a situation where that individual or guest who had a bad experience with an usher bumps into the same usher at the neighborhood grocery store? Well, what do you know? Didn't quite think about that happening. Well, it just did and now what? Does the usher say hello? Does the usher pretend he didn't recognize the individual? Either way, it's highly unlikely this meeting will be a comfortable one for either party. The word awkward comes to mind.

The preferred scenario is where both parties are glad to see each other and able to exchange pleasantries, but this scenario can only find its foundation from the first point of contact at church and how it was handled. The bulk of the responsibility in this regard falls on the shoulders of the usher, who is an ambassador of the church and who is duty bound to make the right impression, not for the sake of being simply impressive, but so that Jesus Christ is represented well through him or her. If an usher is abrasive, no matter how wonderful the sermon was and how many people responded to the altar call, more often than not, all the aggrieved individual remembers and shares with anyone who cares to listen is the obnoxious and offensive usher. While you can't always control this, do your part to ensure you have "clean hands" concerning each interaction and surrender the rest to God and let Him be your advocate.

Two experiences come to mind which could have been a "make or break" experience. The first experience involves my family and I as guests at a friend's church about fifteen years ago, when my younger son was an infant. It was a revival service. I can't recall how we were ushered in and seated, but I do remember my younger son wanted to play with a toy which my wife didn't feel was appropriate at the time and whispered to him that he could play with it later. As is typical for a child of that age, that didn't go down too well with him and he became emotional and started sobbing, not loudly, but it looked like he was either trying to stop himself from crying or revving up to unleash that big crying scream that babies seem to specialize in. I'm not sure which one it would have been, but there was a female usher close by who had apparently been watching all of this unfold. In the twinkle of an eye, while my wife was trying to console our son, the usher came to us rather regimentally and said "You have to take him out now. Come with me..."or something to that effect. My wife and I obliged and followed her instruction. She took us to a nursery where we left our son while we went back to the service.

There was absolutely nothing wrong with her request. The only problem was with the way it was presented. It wasn't cordial, neither was there an explanation or information provided regarding the availability of a nursery when we walked in. If we use the scenario of the flustered mother in a prior chapter above, my wife and I could have been upset with how the situation was handled, but thankfully, because we both have experience in matters such as this, we were able to see beyond how we were approached and focus more on the need to ensure the service was not interrupted and the purpose we attended the service in the first place.

The second scenario was a Wednesday midweek service at CIC, about five years ago. I noticed a gentleman come in and clearly recognized it was his first time at the church. I make it my responsibility (as it should be) to make sure all first time guests are welcomed, seated, and made comfortable. There must be a consistency in doing this without favor or preference given to anyone. Let me be more direct with this: just because someone arrives driving a Bentley should not make me or anyone else treat him or her like a celebrity then halfheartedly welcome the individual who walks in unshaved and somewhat scruffy. Unfortunately, this kind of judging, preferential treatment to be specific, exists in churches. It behooves church leadership to ensure this type of behavior, if it exists, is eradicated with a firm decisiveness.

Back to the Wednesday service; I introduced myself and welcomed the gentleman. He informed me he had recently relocated to Florida from another state. As is our practice for our "Wednesday Impact Prayer and Praise" meetings we end by taking prayer requests from anyone who has one to share, and we pray for the needs accordingly. The gentleman (initials F.M. now having met him) shared a prayer request for his sick mother, asking for God's healing touch. F.M. visited the church one more Wednesday and I inquired about his mother, calling her by her name, because I made it a point to journal her name so I could remember to pray for her. He was pleasantly surprised that not only did I ask how she was feeling, but that I also remembered her name. I didn't think it was a big deal, because I felt it was the proper thing to do. That was the last we saw of him, until I bumped into him at a neighborhood gas station where we exchanged pleasantries and he informed me he was attending another church that conducted services in Spanish.

We exchanged phone numbers, saying we would keep in touch with each other. Interestingly enough, I kept bumping into him at this same gas station, and I would always ask how his mom was doing.

On one occasion, he informed me his mother had passed away and was now with the Lord. I expressed my condolences and this was when he made some remarks that will forever remain heartwarming for me. He started by saying there was no time he drove by CIC that he didn't say a prayer for me and my family; he stated that as he prays for me, he is led to also pray for the church as a whole; he expressed deep gratitude for the way I welcomed him the first time he attended CIC and that He would never forget that. I was moved with emotions and fought back tears because I just couldn't see anything that

The seemingly little things matter.

was spectacular in the way I welcomed him. I do know I welcomed him with God's love, and with respect, as with everybody else, and I do this, asking God to help me show His love at all times. The seemingly little things matter. I firmly believe people can sense and feel the difference—a genuine, authentic welcome, or one that is merely procedural, as a matter of course and as such, mechanical in nature, lacking warmth or love.

I share this not to be self-serving or to give myself a pat on the back, but to sincerely show that it makes a difference how ushers approach their responsibilities and the crucial necessity of doing everything with humility and love. These are uncompromisingly vital for the success and victory of the ministry, to facilitate the work of God in the church and for the overall wellness of the church. Toward ushering (as with everything else that pertains to the church) the motivation must be right. It has to be and can only be the desire to be of service to the glory of God; to be used as God's vessel in being an agent of light. You may be the only reason one individual is able to smile for the whole day, simply because of your loving and authentic welcome. Never underestimate the value and importance of this in ministry and in service to the church. F.M. and I remain in contact to date and he periodically texts me inspirational scripture and words of encouragement, which on several occasions have been just what I needed to uplift my spirit.

CHAPTER EIGHT

LET'S MAKE A MARKED DIFFERENCE

The intent and expectation in writing this book is not to recommend a one size fits all approach for church ushering. As already acknowledged, every church has its own DNA, however, all that is done should be done in love—agape love, so that God's name is glorified through everything that transpires. The hope is that this book provides more insight into the ministry of ushering and how indispensable it is to the continued healthy growth of the church. Prayerfully, every reader is able to capture and envision areas where improvements can be made, or practices implemented toward augmenting what already exists by way of church policy or protocol. Humility and accountability to God and church leadership should stir our spirits to yield to the truth that regardless of how long we've known the Lord, served the Lord, and regardless of the depth of experience we have in ministry, including academic/theological accreditations, we can't know it all. There is always room to learn, improve and also benefit from those who may not know as much as we do. I find it essential to be fluid to the movement and prompting of the Holy Spirit, rather than anchor one's perspective in a rigid mindset. Growth spiritually should also involve our ability to adjust, as circumstances require, all within the framework of God's Word and the leading of the Holy Spirit.

The Bible lets us know that God remembers we are flesh (Psalm 78:39). We may try, but we can't attain perfection in our mortal frames. Only by God's grace are we able to do anything; so our mindset should never be to function in our own stride, but solely by letting Him work in and through us, as yielded vessels, for His glory.

In each of us, He has deposited and invested in spiritual gifts. No longer should these gifts be dormant or ineffective. Not for self-acclaim or public recognition, but because these gifts are not ours to keep.

In each of us, He has deposited and invested in spiritual gifts. No longer should these gifts be dormant or ineffective. Not for self-acclaim or public recognition, but because these gifts are not ours to keep. The world needs these gifts, so that as they are activated in us, by our yieldedness and obedience to the Holy Spirit, the Great Commission is fulfilled through us, God's chosen vessels. To all we do, there must be an essence. Why do we do what we do? There must be a compelling reason; otherwise each action is carried out in vacuum or futility, without a focus or purpose. Let's consider what may seem basic or mundane—brushing our teeth, for example. Like it or not, without brushing your teeth, they will rot and the anguish of pain from cavities tops the chart in terms of discomfort, besides every other hygienic reason why it makes good sense to brush our teeth.

Likewise, there has to be an essence – a compelling reason why we serve or hold any position in the church. A distinction must be made between circular positions in our everyday workplaces in comparison to positions held in church. As followers of Christ, we are to lead by example, serving, to be used as a vessel of God, and not to arrogate to ourselves authority we don't have and maybe sometimes shouldn't have, if it's being used abusively, arrogantly, or oppressively. We have to be part of the equation that attracts and draws people closer to God, or in any event, so function in our daily lifestyle that people are attracted to us and gravitate toward us, because they just need to know what makes us different in how we handle matters. This becomes the ministry opportunity to share the Good News and talk about the influence of Jesus Christ in your personal life. This is the essence of why we are Christians and why we worship and honor God in all we do and strive to do.

I always feel a spur within me anytime I remember that not only did Jesus pay the full price for my salvation, but that others paved the way toward this; to ensure I heard the Good News, not only martyrs in the Bible, but everyone who invested their time to witness to me, invite me to a church service or event, or sent me devotionals to reflect upon. I am duty bound to do the same—every believer is. Remember the Words of Christ in Matthew 5:14-16:

"You are the light of the world. A city that is set on a hill cannot be hidden. Nor do they light a lamp and put it under a basket, but on a lampstand, and it gives light to all who are in the house. Let your light so shine before men, that they may see your good works and glorify your Father in heaven." (NKJV)

USHERING IN HIS PRESENCE
Tribute Song

"Use Me for Your Glory" © 2020

Use me, Lord, for your glory

Use me, Lord, for your praise

Use me, Lord, for your glory

Use me, Lord, I am yours

I am yours, oh Lord

I am yours, oh Lord

I am yours, oh Lord

Use me now

I am yours, oh Lord

I am yours, oh Lord

I am yours, oh Lord

Use me now

Use me Lord for your glory

Use me Lord for your praise

Use me Lord for your glory

Use me Lord I am yours

-Olanrewaju Asiru

ABOUT THE AUTHOR

Olanrewaju (Lanre) Asiru is originally from Lagos, Nigeria, and has a background in law, with a Master's from the Franklin Pierce Law Center, Concord, New Hampshire. From a very young age, Lanre has always had a heart to serve and deep compassion for the underprivileged and abused. His heart's desire is to be a vessel in helping people come to a full understanding of who they are in Christ. Lanre serves in various capacities at Catalyst International Church, including his role as the Head Usher. Lanre and his wife, Adenike, are blessed with two sons, Oluwatobiloba and Oluwafeyishayo.

IF YOU'RE A FAN OF THIS BOOK, WILL YOU HELP ME SPREAD THE WORD?

There are several ways you can help me get the word out about the message of this book…

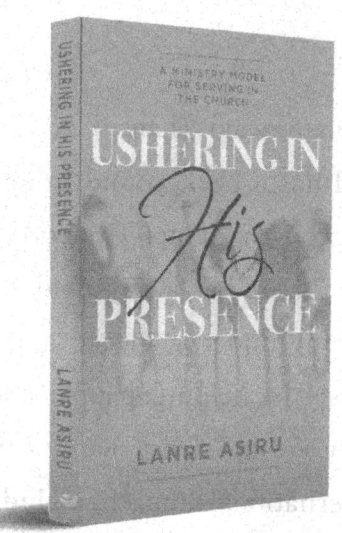

- Post a 5-Star review on Amazon.

- Write about the book on your Facebook, Twitter, Instagram, LinkedIn, – any social media you regularly use!

- If you blog, consider referencing the book, or publishing an excerpt from the book with a link back to my website at **www.lanreasiru.com**. You have my permission to do this as long as you provide proper credit and backlinks.

- Recommend the book to friends – word-of-mouth is still the most effective form of advertising.

- Purchase additional copies to give away as gifts.

Visit my Website at: www.lanreasiru.com
The best way to connect with me is by email
at **lasiru@lanreasiru.com**.